TOY POODLE

Puppy Guide

TOY POODLE Puppy Guide

SIDNEY WAYNE MIDDLETON II

TATE PUBLISHING
AND ENTERPRISES, LLC

Published by Tate Publishing & Enterprises, LLC
127 E. Trade Center Terrace | Mustang, Oklahoma 73064 USA
1.888.361.9473 | www.tatepublishing.com

Tate Publishing is committed to excellence in the publishing industry. The company reflects the philosophy established by the founders, based on Psalm 68:11,
"The Lord gave the word and great was the company of those who published it."

Cover & interior design by Lindsay B. Behrens
Illustrations by Noelle Barcelo

Published in the United States of America

ISBN: 978-1-62295-810-8
1. Pets / Dogs / Breeds
13.04.23

TABLE OF CONTENTS

In loving memory
Sidney Wayne Middleton II

WHY A TOY POODLE

If you want a breed that is beautiful, very smart, easy to train, clean, non-shedding, non-smelly, easy to get along with, a good house dog, a watchdog, and a good retriever, then the poodle is the breed for you.

They have long life spans of fifteen to twenty years. Toy poodles tend to usually be very robust till the very end.

The only drawback to the poodle breed is the regular grooming needed and that they just might be smarter than you!

Poodles are not sissy dogs. I know it is hard to get past the fluffy, fu-fu exterior, but there are various different poodle hair clips to choose from. Virtually anything you can imagine you can do with a poodle's coat. Many talented groomers that compete will use poodles for their cuts as the coat is nice and dense and curly and will hold any cut that you put it into and is very easy to hand scissor and sculpt.

The poodle was bred as a water retrieval dog. They love the water, just like the Labs and golden retrievers, and can retrieve just as well.

Poodles are very versatile. They do well in conformation, agility, fly ball, and obedience. Poodles (standard and miniature) are being used as search-and-rescue dogs, handicap assistance dogs, mobility assistance dogs, and Seeing Eye dogs. The toy poodles are being used as therapy dogs, cancer alert dogs, blood sugar alert dogs, and seizure alert dogs. They also excel at being loving, loyal pets in the home.

Remember that any animal that you decide on is a lifelong commitment, and they need to be treated just like babies for the rest of their lives as they cannot tell you (in voice) what is wrong with them.

THINGS YOU SHOULD KNOW ABOUT BREEDERS

Not all breeders are breeders. There are several types that need to be mentioned.

Registered breeders AKC, UKC, NKC, CKC, APRI, etc.: These are breeders that breed their dogs to improve the breed and to pass a quality dog to new owners. These breeders are registered with the kennel clubs of their breed. (Just because your puppy is registered does not mean you are a registered breeder.) These breeders breed their dogs to the standards of the kennel club(s) that they belong to and are registered with their kennel clubs as breeders. They do not sell their puppies to pet stores as their dogs are top quality dogs and they do not want to be associated with puppy mill–buying pet stores.

Puppy mills breeders: These are people that keep their animals in cages without much human contact. They breed only for the money and do not care about you or the animals that they are breeding. They have also been known to mix their breeds and sell the animals off as purebreds.

> Puppy mills have been around for decades. They continue to thrive because they prey on unwitting consumers who are smitten by too-cute-for-words puppies in pet store windows and on legitimate-seeming websites. Puppy mills house dogs in shockingly poor conditions. After their fertility wanes, breeding animals are often killed, abandoned or sold cheaply to another mills to try and get "one more litter" out of the dog. The annual results of all this breeding is millions of puppies, many with behavior and/or health problems.
>
> (SPCA)

Maw and paw breeders: These are people that have a dame, and they want to breed their baby so she can have puppies. Either to get another female or to make some extra money. In this case, you must be sure to talk to both sire and dame owners. Most of these people have no concept of how to properly breed or what colors goes with what, they just breed. Very few show quality dogs come from this type of breeding, but a good place to get a pet.

QUESTIONS THAT YOU NEED TO ASK THE SELLER

1 Are you a breeder? How long have you been breeding dogs?
2. How often do you breed a litter with the same dame?
3. Do you consider this a business or a hobby?
4. Why did you breed this litter?
5. What do you like or dislike about this breed?
6. What breed traits might not make this breed the right choice for me or my family?
7. What are your requirements for new owners?
8. Do you pick the puppy, or do I get to choose from all or some of the puppies?
9. What are the health issues in this breed?
10. Where do you raise your puppies?
11. What do you feed your puppies?
12. What are the parents like?
13. Are the mother and father on the premises? If not, where can I find the sire's owner?
14. Are there any other relatives I could see?
15. Do you offer a contract or sales agreement? If so, what are the terms?
16. Do you offer a health guarantee and what does it cover?
17. What health checks are done, on the parents and the puppies?
18. Will you supply a veterinary health clearance certification?
19. Will you supply the pedigree and registration when we take the puppy home?
20. Have any vaccines been given, and what will be needed once puppy leaves?
21. What was the date of the last worming?
22. What kind of training is required?
23. Are you available for long-time help with training or behavior questions or problems?
24. Will you provide the puppies medical records, worming/shots, and any other medical history?

MIDDLETON'S TOY POODLES

We breed only toy poodles and have been since 1979.

We fell in love with these remarkable toy poodles and were not sure what to do or how to train or care for him as he was our first toy poodle. We went to our local veterinary clinic and got some information, but it was very general. We started a strict health regiment on our baby, then when he was a year old, we decided to get him a mate. When we had our first litter, again, we had to contact our veterinarian. I also contacted AKC and was given some breeder's phone number to contact. I got some good advice from the veterinarians and AKC poodle breeders. (There was no Internet then and finding this information took a long time nor were there very many books available.)

We breed our toy poodles in our home and maintain them there as well. They are a part of the family and need loving, care, and interaction, just as we all do. Maintaining and breeding in a home is better and easier than having the babies out in a kennel facility, but it still requires a lot of work and requires a lot of sanitizing and maintenance.

We ensure that the puppies you get from us are healthy and up-to-date on all worming and shots either through our veterinarian or by the medication that has been prescribed for them, with follow-ups by the veterinarian. We will also provide you with a health certificate upon request. We also request that you have you baby checked out by a veterinarian within a week. This is due to the medication that they are required to take weekly until they are twelve weeks old.

We do follow-ups with all of our babies (via e-mail, phone, or by mail) that we have placed in new homes. I feel that this is important, both for us and the new owner. I am always pleased to hear that they are doing fine and are very smart and that they are on a continued health program.

We also have a contract that you must agree to and sign before we will place our toy poodles into your care. On this contract is our warranty on the health and fitness of our toy poodles.

We provide you with some important guidelines on how to take care of your new puppy and encourage you to give us feedback so that we can improve on the information that we provide. So now that I have been getting a lot of requests for additional information, I have put a toy poodle puppy guide together and this is its result.

I have been gathering information on toy poodle puppies from other breeders and through my own experience for over twenty years. I know how important it is to have the correct information on hand and how frustrating it is when you're unable to find it. You can buy books but will not have a book on just poodle puppies from *A* to *Z*. Then you have to buy a book on grooming, but it is general and covers a lot of the other animals and does not give specific details on just one breed. You can buy a book on poodles, and there again, it talks briefly on puppies and does not go into much details on poodle puppy raising. Then there is the book on breeding your dog. (I have left out breeding as I am only talking about the poodle puppy.) However, I have included all of the AKC/UKC/CKC/NKC poodle clips you can use throughout your baby's life. I have included some information on showing your AKC puppy. Who knows your baby could be the next champion. Get a lot of ribbons, they have it in them.

Last and very important, toy Poodles are two inches and under. No teacup and no tiny toy poodles. If they are under ten inches they are toy poodles: AKC, CKC, NKC and UKC as well as European kennel clubs all list toy poodles and nothing smaller. So do not be sold on any other description.

MALE VERSUS FEMALE

(an age-old debate)

I realize that each person has their individual preference, and each dog has its own personality, but you should never count out a male. If it were up to me and I was not a breeder, I would have all males.

People often want females because they are more laid-back than males. I have to say that is totally bogus. Most of the time, the male is easier going than the female as females are usually the leaders of the pack. They tend to be bossier than the males and more independent. The males will never stake a claim on a certain area of the bed or a favorite toy: he will play with whatever he can find first. The females like to control their toys and spots on the beds. Also, I have seen the females mark their territory by peeing in the house and the male gets blamed for it. Females can also be horribly moody, going from happy to ornery in just a flash of seconds. Remember, there is a reason they call girls bitches. Also, on top of all that, you have the cycles (twice a year for thirty days each) of the female to deal with, if not spayed. This can be very messy and time-consuming as you have to guard your female extra carefully during this time if you are not breeding them. Also, in most cases you can plan on spending more $$$$ on a female because of their breeding capabilities.

Males on the other hand are very loyal and protective and bond very well to you. They are less territorial than females are and can adapt much more quickly than a female to new situations. If a male is neutered early or trained carefully, they will not lift their legs. This seems to be the most common complaint I hear about males. I have had many males and I have had them all together in the house (no females). None of them lifted their legs to mark on anything in the house because we trained them not to. It is not as hard as people make it out to be. Now outside is another matter as full intact males will lift their leg and mark their territory. Males do very well together as long as there is no female in the house.

As far as a difference between males and females when it comes to activity level, the males want to play and exercise more than their female counterparts, but there isn't a whole lot of other differences. Now when it comes to taking them for a walk in the park, they are all ready for a new adventure. Some poodles are couch potatoes and some live to get up and go. This has to do with the home environment that they are being raised in, and that should be more of a factor than the basis on the sex of the puppy. All animals adapt to the living conditions of the owners.

SOME HISTORY

The toy poodle was the result of inbreeding in France to bring down the size of the animal; whether this was done on purpose or not, we are not sure. While the standard poodle was bred as a water dog, the miniature and toy Poodles were strictly companion dogs popular in the French court from the reign of Louis XIV through that of Louis XVI. Miniature and toy poodles appear in many seventeenth century paintings. These dogs were also popular circus performers with clowns as early as the 1700s through today. Poodles were first brought the United States in the early nineteenth century. The first poodle registered in the United States was in 1896 with the American Kennel Club (AKC), which had been established in 1884 in Philadelphia.

This breed was popular with the aristocrats of New York City in the early twentieth century and did not become popular until after WWII. By the midfifties, the miniature and toy poodles were the most sought after dog in the United States, a position that is still held today. There are three breeds recognized by all the kennel clubs throughout the globe: the standard, miniature, and toy.

Standard Poodle - Over 15" / 38cm

Miniature Poodle - Over 10" / 25.4cm to 15" / 38cm

Toy Poodles - 10" / 25.4cm and under

The poodle (all three breeds) is a high maintenance dog and cannot be raised like other dogs; they require grooming (bath and clips) every four to six weeks and require an exercise regimen.

GENERAL APPEARANCE

The toy poodle is a small squarely built dog with a distinctive harsh curly coat that may be presented in any of several traditional poodle clips or corded. The ears are long, drop, and densely feathered. The tail is normally docked, set high, and carried erect. The length of the body (sternum to point of buttocks) is equal to the height (withers to ground). The poodle carries him/herself with an air of dignity and pride.

CHARACTERISTIC

The poodle's most readily identifiable characteristic is its harsh dense coat, which is presented in a various traditional trims. Another essential characteristic is proper temperament. The breed is noted for its high intelligence and trainability. While poodles are wary of strangers, they require human companionship and do not do well without regular close interaction with family members. Because of their great intelligence and the joy that they take in human companionship, MAKE THE Poodle one of the most sought after dogs in the world. Poodles excel in performance events of all sorts. They are extremely affectionate (male or female) with children.

TEMPERAMENT

The toy poodle is good-natured and eager-to-please. He's also cheerful, loyal, proud, dignified, and extremely smart. When most people think of a poodle, they think of a feminine girl dog. But nothing could be further from than the truth. He's actually very rugged and athletic. He's incredibly intelligent—one of the most intelligent breeds—and is easily trained. He thinks of himself as a person and demands to be treated like one. He's very affectionate and craves your love and companionship. He wants to be with you always. He's highly playful and loves to clown around. He possesses a keen sense of humor! He's highly energetic and very active around the home. He's playful and can learn to play fetch! He's a strong swimmer and loves the water. He's highly social and loves all people. He's gentle and patient with children. He gets along well with other dogs and pets. If he's bored, he will get into mischief, so you need to give him something to do to occupy his mind. He house-trains easily. He's one of the most popular breeds.

GENERAL INFORMATION

EXERCISE

Toy poodles are an easy dog to exercise. Most of the exercise they need they get while playing in the yard or in the house. Poodles do love to run though, so be careful, they can get away from you. They also love to play, so be sure to provide plenty of toys to play with so they do not mistake furniture and other household items as chew toys.

SOCIALIZATION

Toy poodles can sometimes be shy and timid (mostly due to their extremely small size), it is very important that you take time to socialize with your new puppy with kids and other pets that are in your home. If not properly socialized, your puppy could become nippy and aggressive out of fear. Puppies get important socialization from their mother and human contact during the first six to eight weeks of their life. Go slow when introducing your new puppy to children and other pets. Never force a relationship. This can cause the exact opposite of what you wish to accomplish.

OBEDIENCE

Toy poodles are very smart, eager to please, and easy to train. In fact, they are used in the circus today and years past because they are able to learn many tricks and are very agile. Books can be a great way to learn to train your puppy, or you can take an obedience class at your local pet training center. It is as important for a dog to have good manners as well as people. No one likes a disobedient dog! It can be fun for both you and your puppy. You will be amazed at what you can learn to do with a little training and a lot of patience.

FEEDING

Do not feed your puppy soft canned food for very long. The chewing of hard food helps to keep teeth clean and healthy. Canned food can also cause your puppy to become overweight. Try not to change your puppy's food diet unless absolutely necessary. It can hurt your puppy's digestive system and can also cause diarrhea. Puppies need to be fed four times a day. As your puppy ages, the number of feedings can be reduced to two times a day. A feeding just before bedtime helps your puppy to sleep better. I recommend that you follow the feeding directions on the back of your dog food bag.

The food we feed our mothers and puppies is Blue Buffalo Life Protection Formula puppy. Please do not feed your puppy human food! Dog food has everything your puppy needs for proper nutrition.

HEALTH

Please remember your puppies' regular immunizations. These are essential to good health. Especially parvo shots. Beware! Some small dogs have adverse reaction to the chemicals in the shots. However, we have never lost a dog from an immunization, and this is not an excuse to not have immunizations. Most puppies just become lethargic and may have some diarrhea. This usually resolves itself within twenty-four to forty-eight hours. If your vet will use a five-in-one shot instead of a seven-in-one shot, this should solve the problem. Please let your vet know beforehand. Remember, if your puppy should become sick at any time, please do not wait too long to see your vet.

FROM PREGNANCY TO YOUR HOME

Preparing for Babies' Arrival

During the mother's pregnancy, we have her checked out by our veterinarian. This is to make sure that she is still in good health and able to carry the puppies full term (sixty-three days). Here, she will receive any medication to help her along the way. We then start her on high-protein puppy food. This helps her in several ways: it provides the necessary calcium she will need for her bones and the puppies, and it provides her with the protein needed for her milk. At fifty to fifty-six days into her pregnancy, we have her X-rayed. This is to ensure that the babies are the right size for her to deliver and to get a puppy count. In some rare cases, toy poodles puppies have reverted back to their original breed size. (This would mean that we would have to have a C-section.) Once we have confirmed that we can proceed with the babies she is carrying, we help her get her birth place ready. This is important to her as she will want to make sure that there are no intruders or other animals that can get in to her babies.

Puppy's Arrival

We are there to help her in the delivery of her puppies and to make sure that they are all breathing and whining. We then clean each newborn and put them with their mother and under a towel. Once she has delivered the entire litter of puppies, we will then clean her up with a damp cloth and get her back with her babies. (She is a very proud mother at this point and very tired too.) We call and set up a tail docking and declawing appointment with our veterinary clinic. We keep a close watch on the puppies and mother for the next twenty-four hours to ensure that all the puppies are in good shape.

Three Days Old

At three days old, they get their first examination: tail docking, declawing, and blood work are conducted. Once the puppies have been cleared and are found to be in good health, the vet will give a prescription for babies and mother. This is where worming medication and instructions are given. The vet will also tell you that it is very important that the babies suckle for at least three weeks as the milk they receive has all the antibiotic necessary to fight off any parasites that could endanger the puppies.

Seven to Twenty-Four Days Old

The mother will keep the area where the puppies are cleaned of any body waste that the puppies produce until they start eating from a dish. We keep the bedding washed and remove it daily. Sanitizing the area daily is just as important as keeping the bedding cleaned. We start their worming when they are two weeks old and thereafter until they are twelve weeks old. Should you get a puppy before it is twelve weeks old, you must continue providing your baby with the same worming medication.

When the babies are fourteen days old, they are moving around on all fours quite well, and we start interacting with them; they are able to hear quite well at this age and their eyes are open, but they are still trying to get focused. We also start training them on simple commands and praising them, "Come" and "Good boy/girl." They receive lots of TLC.

They also train you to come to their barks and whining, just like a real baby does.

Twenty-Five and Up

When the puppies are twenty-five days old, we start feeding them out of the dish with a mixture of canned and dry puppy chow with water mixed in. Once they get started, they really go for it. We feed them twice a day while the mother is still feeding them twice a day. Once the puppies are thirty-two days old, we feed them three times a day with less wet dog food and more dry, while the mother feeds them once a day. When they are thirty-six days old, they are just getting fed from the dish with dry dog food with water. The mother has not stopped letting them suckle. When the puppies are forty-two days of age, they eat nothing but dry dog food and drinking water from different bowls.

At the beginning of their fourth week, we start taking them outside to allow them to play and get the feel of the grass. Here, they follow their mother and are very observant in watching their mother. They learn to go potty outside, and we continue to take them out after each feeding.

When they are four weeks of age, we start teaching them some basic commands: come, sit, dance, bark, and beg. We do this with treats. Then when the puppies are six weeks old, they are ready to go to a new home.

When they turn six weeks old, we provide them with their first parvovirus shots. These shots are required every three weeks until they reach the age of six months. Your veterinarian will provide you with a medication program that you will need to stick to.

Things You Need to Do before You Pick Up Your Puppy

1. Find a veterinarian and talk with him/her; ask questions and get comfortable with him/her. It is just like you have a doctor that you trust and believe in.
2. Ask the breeder what type of food he is feeding the puppies.
3. Decide what type of house (potty) training you are going to do.
4. Food and water dishes, stainless steel or ceramic. (No plastic as it has harmful toxins that could cause your puppy to become sick.) Decide where you want the puppy to eat. Make sure it is out of the way of traffic.
5. Bedding (there are several good choices). Some stuffed toys or make some old sock about the same size as the puppy. He/she is used to sleeping with its siblings and having these items will help it and you sleep better at night.
6. Puppy's quiet place, a place that it can go to rest and feel secure.
7. Find yourself a good groomer; we provide our puppies with their first puppy cut, but most of breeders do not. You puppy needs grooming every six to eight weeks. Ask the groomer lots of questions before you trust them with you puppy.

Preparing for a puppy is a lot of work, but the rewards you will receive after you have everything in place will be well worth it.

THE FIRST FORTY-EIGHT HOURS

Finally, it is time to bring your new puppy home. Here are a few preparations that you may need to go through to get ready for that new baby.

Create a safe, friendly environment.

1. Make sure that all poisonous items are out of puppies' reach.
2. Remove any poisonous plants.
3. Look at your home from your new puppies' point of view and remove any hazardous items that could cause problems (electric cords, bobby pins, etc.).

There are things that your new puppy will need :

1. Food and water dish. Stainless steel or ceramic. No plastic.
2. A collar and a leash. Collars for the toy poodle puppy are generally cat collars.
3. A metal pin brush for fluffing and a nice metal comb (poodle comb). Brushes are great for surface brushing, but you really need a comb for getting the mats out and getting down to the skin.
4. Safe and appropriate toys. Usually, if a toy can fit comfortably in a puppy's mouth, it is too small.
5. A travel crate for sleeping in. Large enough for puppies' growth and comfort.
6. A gate that can keep your puppy confined to an area. They will seek ways of escaping, so make sure it is escape proof.
7. Wee-Wee pads. They make potty training much easier on you and your new puppy.

Puppies should be fed three to four times a day. The toy poodle breed does not gulp down their food, but nibbles on it. My toy poodles are fed twice a day of one cup dry dog food per animal. These babies only consume one-fourth cup of dry dog food a day. As they get older, they will increase their intake. Feed in same location daily.

PUPPY'S NEW HOME

You have picked up your new puppy, and you are excited. The puppy is nervous and scared as he/she is now in a new environment that he does not know. He is also excited about his new adventures that await him.

Once you get him to his new home, you need to let him outside for a short while to allow him to potty; this could take up to thirty minutes. Then take him inside and place him in his bedding area and let him explore the surroundings. Go to the food area that you have set up for him and start calling him by the name that you are giving him. Let him come to you as this will start his training on your commands to come when you call.

Once the puppy has eaten, have him follow you outside, within fifteen minutes, and stay with him and let him go potty. Praise him and give him a small treat, let him play if he wants to, then have him follow you back into the house. (I do not feed my puppies after 6:00 p.m.) If you are in an area where you can leave the door open to allow him to go in and out, that will help a lot; he will enjoy the freedom and will learn faster to go potty outside. That brings up a point that needs to be addressed here: if he can go in and out, make sure that you have an eye on him at all times. He will start going to the door and letting you know that he needs to go potty or he wants to go outside to play. This will happen between the age of three to four months on males and five to six months on females.

Once bedtime comes around, you need to make sure he cannot roam around the house. If he is able to do this, you will have several surprises (a small baby pen or a travel crate are some good items to use). Again, this is going to happen as they are still babies and cannot control themselves. (At about four months, their bladder will be fully formed, and they should be able to hold it all night long.) When you get up the next morning, you need to take the puppy outside; again, have him follow you. This begins a routine for him and one that he will adapt to very fast.

VETERINARIAN APPOINTMENT

Your puppy will be up-to-date on vaccination and worming. You will receive all shot and worming records to take to your veterinarian. Your veterinarian will continue a vaccination schedule, which you must follow up with. Puppies get a series of vaccinations, just like children go through immunizations. It is typically a series of parvo shots until they are six months old. All pups are born with roundworms, so we start worming at two weeks, then weekly. They will need this until they are twelve weeks. They should not have any worms by the time they are in your care. That is why we insist that you have your puppy checked by your veterinarian within a few days. Also, annual dental care is a must for the lifelong health of your puppy.

TRAINING

There are options to choose from when it comes to training your new toy poodle puppy. Here are a few options: crate train, another is to train the puppy to go potty on a pad (Wee-Wee pad or puppy training pad), or newspaper and litter box training. Here are some useful links to help you decide how you want to potty train your puppy.

http://www.tonypassera.com/thedogsite
http://www.barkbyter.com/training/crate.htm
http://www.bichon.org/crate.htm

DOS AND DON'TS

Do No matter what way you choose to train your poodle, be sure to always praise your puppy and give it a treat when the job is well done. Using a stern lower voice is enough scolding to the toy poodle.

Don't Please do not harm your puppy in any way when getting frustrated in training. Remember, they are only going to learn if you are consistent in teaching them. So many people give up or do not try hard enough to properly train a dog. A poodle is one of the most intelligent breeds out there, and they are not difficult to train if you are consistent.

Do Puppies sleep a lot so make sure you have an area designated just for him/her. A blanket, towel, or doggy bed in the corner of a room will work just fine. If you are crate training your puppy, the crate will do just fine. (Once crate training is complete, you can remove the door and the puppy's crate will be a safe place for it to rest/sleep. Crates should not be too big nor too small, just enough room for him/her to stand up and turn around when grown.

Don't Children should be supervised when playing with puppies. If a puppy is mistreated, it could change that puppy's personality for the rest of his/her life! Make sure that the puppy is never left unattended with any children you are unsure of. Some children are respectful of animals, and as we all know, some are never taught to be respectful.

Don't As we all know, toy poodles are very popular dogs. Never leave your toy poodle unattended outdoors. I have actually had customers call me and report their dog was stolen from their yard! Do not take any chances; keep a watchful eye on your toy poodle no matter his/her age. Also be careful of large birds. Eagles, hawks, and owls—these birds will swoop down and grab your toy poodle. That has happened to a breeder friend of mine. She lost two of her breeding dogs to hawks.

Don't Lastly, do not let your puppy walk anywhere in the public that an ill animal could have been until they are fully vaccinated. This usually means at least six months of age. Once they have all of their vaccinations in them, they are usually immune to the diseases. Public parks, stores that allow you to bring your pets in, and vet clinics are the main places to be careful of. At the vet clinic, make sure that the examination room is clean before you put your puppy down on the table or floor. You can never be too safe in these matters, and the vet will respect you for this.

FEEDING YOUR PUPPY

After you receive your puppy, you should continue to feed them with the food that has been provided to you by your breeder. Should your breeder not provide you any food, then ask what puppy food they have been feeding them. This is important as a change could result in diarrhea and a loss of appetite. I use the Blue Buffalo puppy food for all my puppies now.

Should you decide to change the puppy's diet, then this must be done gradually. Use the dog food that it is used to eating and mix it with the brand that you have decided on (first week, 3/4 old to 1/4 new, second week 1/2 to 1/2, third 1/4 to ¾, and in the fourth week, all new.) This allows for the puppy's system to adjust to the new food without incidents.

Feeding your toy poodle should not be a hassle as they will eat about 1 cup to 1-1/2 cup dry dog food a day. If you set it out for feeding and then pick it up after he has eaten, check the amount he has eaten. Some toy poodles eat like cats, a little at a time, and it could take twenty-four hours for them to eat it all. This is okay, nothing to be alarmed with. That is how my dogs eat. They run and play take a nap, then grab a quick bite and repeat their daily routine.

Storing your dry dog food is important. It should be kept in a container with a cover/lid over it. This will help prevent other unwanted animals from helping themselves to your baby's food and from contaminating it. Leaving it in the bag in the closet is only inviting varmints.

HUMAN FOODS THAT ARE HARMFUL TO YOUR DOG

Alcoholic drinks - can cause intoxication and death (liquor, beer, and wine)
Apple cores - choking hazard
Apricot pits - choking hazard
Avocado leaves, fruit, bark, and seeds - toxic
Baby food that contains onion powder - onion powder is toxic
Bone of fish and poultry - choking or lacerations due to the bones splintering
Broccoli - toxic
Cat food - too high in fats and proteins
Chocolate - toxic
Cigarettes, tobacco, and cigars - toxic
Citrus oil extracts - causes vomiting
Coffee and coffee grounds - toxic
Fat trimmings - pancreatitis
Garlic - toxic
Grapes - toxic
Hops - panting, increased heart rate, seizures, and death
Human vitamins that contain iron - toxic
Macadamia nuts - toxic
Moldy and spoiled foods - toxic
Mushrooms - toxic
Onions - toxic
Pear pips - choking
Persimmons - choking hazard and intestinal blockage
Plum pits - choking
Peach pits - choking
Pork chop bones - splinters and cause choking
Potato peelings - toxic
Raisins - toxic
Raw eggs - can cause salmonella
Raw fish - causes a vitamin B deficiency
Rhubarb leaves - toxic
Raw salmon - toxic
Salt - can lead to an electrolyte imbalance in large amounts
Sugar - obesity
Sugarless candies - toxic
Tomato leaves and stems - toxic
Yeast dough - the gas gets trapped in the digestive system causing major problems
Xylitol - ingredient found in chewing gum, gumdrops, Tic Tacs, and other sugar-free candies. It is used as a sweetener and is extremely toxic.

POISONOUS HOUSEPLANTS

Amaryllis
Azalea
Bleeding heart
Caladium
Clematis
Daffodil
Daphne
Dieffenbachia
English ivy
Foxglove
Holly
Iris
Ivy
Mistletoe
Morning glory
Narcissus
Oleander
Philodendron
Poinsettia
Potato
Rhododendron
Rubber plant
Sago palm
Tobacco
Tulip
Weeping fig
Yew

HEALTH CONCERNS IN THE TOY POODLE

Patellar Luxation

Is where the kneecap does not fit in the groove of the leg bone properly and causes a popping of the kneecap when the leg is bent. Some dogs with this genetic disease can be seen to limp or jerk the leg up occasionally when running or walking. This disease can be diagnosed by your vet by performing a simple manipulation of the kneecap. Reports can be registered with OFA after one year of age. Dogs found to have luxating patellas should not be bred.

Patent Ductus Arteriosus (PDA)

Is the most common congenital heart defect seen in dogs. The vessel that carries the blood in neonate puppies closes immediately at birth. This disease happens when this vessel does not close at birth. This can cause an overload on the left side of the heart, which causes an enlargement of the left side of the heart. A bounding pulse and heart murmur are signs of this disease. Dogs with this disease should never be bred.

Progressive Retinal Atrophy (PRA)

It causes a breakdown of the tissues at the back of the retina, causing blindness. This is a hereditary disease. You may see a cloudiness of the eyes resulting in cataracts. Dogs can be tested for this at local eye clinics by certified eye specialists. Dogs with this disease should never be bred.

Addison Disease

This disease is caused by the adrenal glands not producing enough cortisone and aldosterone. Symptoms may include decreased appetite, increased thirst, vomiting, diarrhea, and lethargy along with weight loss. The dog will require medication for the rest of its life. Dogs are tested for this disease by a simple blood test. This test does not prove nor disprove carrier status. The dog may test clear, but could still develop the disease later in life and may produce puppies with this disease.

Tearing Toy Poodles

There is no quick fix or easy answer to this question. Being a breeder, I have tried almost everything on the market. I have yet to find a single product that works well enough to warrant the money the product costs. Tearing on toy and some miniature poodles is the norm rather than something unusual. This is due to the tear duct being too small to carry the fluid away from the eye. This does not mean there is something wrong with your poodle or that it is not a purebred or that it is poorly bred like it sounds. Also, the lighter the color of the poodle, the more you will notice the tearing. You may also notice that in the summer some poodles' tearing will increase. This is usually due to an environmental allergy like people have. Sometimes if you notice an increase of the eye tearing along with unusual licking of the dogs' legs or feet or other items in the house, this could be resulting from a food allergy. The best thing to use I have found is nonalcoholic baby wipes.

Canine Parvovirus Infection in Dogs

The canine parvovirus (CPV) infection is a highly contagious viral illness that affects all dogs. The virus manifests itself in two different forms. The more common form is the intestinal form, which is characterized by vomiting, diarrhea, weight loss, and lack of appetite (anorexia). The less common form is the cardiac form, which attacks the heart muscles of very young puppies, often leading to death. The majority of cases are seen in puppies that are between six weeks and six months old. The incidence of canine parvovirus infections have been reduced radically by early vaccination in young puppies.

Symptoms and Types

The major symptoms associated with the intestinal form of a canine parvovirus infection include severe bloody diarrhea, lethargy, anorexia, fever, vomiting, and severe weight loss. The intestinal form of CPV affects the body's ability to absorb nutrients, and an affected animal will quickly become dehydrated and weak from lack of protein and fluid absorption. The wet tissue of the mouth and eyes may become noticeably red and the heart may beat too rapidly. When your veterinarian palpates (examine by touch) your dog's abdominal area, your dog may respond with pain or discomfort. Dogs that have contracted CPV may also have a low body temperature (hypothermia) rather than a fever.

PARVOVIRUS CAUSES

Most cases of CPV infections are caused by a genetic alteration of the original canine parvovirus: the canine parvovirus type 2b. There are a variety of risk factors that can increase a dog's susceptibility to the disease, but mainly, the virus is transmitted either by direct contact with an infected dog or indirectly by the fecal-oral route. Heavy concentrations of the virus are found in an infected dog's stool, so when a healthy dog sniffs an infected dog's stool, it will contract the disease. The virus can also be brought into a dog's environment by way of shoes that have come into contact with infected feces. There is evidence that the virus can live in ground soil for up to a year. It is resistant to most cleaning products or even to weather changes. If you suspect that you have come into contact with feces at all, you will need to wash the affected area with household bleach, the only disinfectant known to kill the virus.

Improper vaccination protocol and vaccination failure can also lead to a CPV infection. Breeding kennels and dog shelters that hold a large number of inadequately vaccinated puppies are particularly hazardous places. For unknown reasons, certain dog breeds such as rottweilers, Doberman pinschers, pit bulls, Labrador retrievers, German shepherds, English springer spaniels, and Alaskan sled dogs are particularly vulnerable to the disease. Diseases or drug therapies that suppress the normal response of the immune system may also increase the likelihood of infection.

Treatment

Since the disease is a viral infection, there is no real cure for it. Treatment is focused on curing the symptoms and preventing secondary bacterial infections, preferably in a hospital environment. Intensive therapy and system support are the keys to recovery. Intravenous fluid and nutrition therapy is crucial in maintaining a dog's normal body fluid after severe diarrhea and dehydration, and protein and electrolyte levels will be monitored and regulated as necessary. Medications that may be used in the treatment include drugs to curb vomiting (antiemetic), H2 blockers to reduce nausea, antibiotics, and anthelmintic to fight parasites. The survival rate in dogs is about 70 percent, but death may sometimes result from severe dehydration, a severe secondary bacterial infection, and bacterial toxins in the blood or a severe intestinal hemorrhage. Prognosis is lower for puppies since they have a less developed immune system. It is common for a puppy that is infected with CPV to suffer shock and sudden death.

Prevention

The best prevention you can take against CPV infection is to follow the correct protocol for vaccination. Young puppies should be vaccinated at six, nine, and twelve weeks and should not be socialized with outside dogs until at least two weeks after their last vaccinations.

CHOCOLATE TOXICITY IN DOGS

Dogs are known for eating things when they are not supposed to. This is especially true of puppies. Also, dogs have an excellent sense of smell, making it fairly easy to find any secret hiding spots for the chocolate. This can be a dangerous combination when there is chocolate around the house.

Chocolate is derived from the roasted seeds of *Theobroma cacao*, which contains certain properties that can be toxic to animals: caffeine and bromine. If ingested, these two ingredients can also lead to various medical complications and may even prove fatal for your dog.

Symptoms and Types

Vomiting
Diarrhea
Increased body temperature
Increased reflex responses
Muscle rigidity
Rapid breathing
Increased heart rate
Low blood pressure
Seizures
Advanced signs (cardiac failure, weakness, and coma)

Three chocolates that a dog should never eat: milk, semisweet, and baking chocolates. 0.3 oz. per pound is dangerous and deadly.

REASONS FOR GROOMING

Grooming is an important part of your toy poodles care. Grooming should be a daily activity. Regular grooming helps to ensure the dog is healthy and comfortable. It is important to note that poodles do not shed and require grooming by a professional groomer every four to six weeks maximum.

The main reasons for daily grooming include:

1. Decreased chance of various health problems, such as thrush, scratches, and other skin problems
2. General cleanliness of the dog.
3. Monitoring of the dog's health by checking for cuts, swelling, lameness, or changes in temperament, all of which could be indicative of illness.
4. Forging of a closer bond between dog and owner.
5. Reducing infestation load of external parasites on skin.

Scissors and clippers:

Cutting tools used to remove/shorten hair on your toy poodle's hair are in sensitive areas. The typical pair of scissors for dog grooming is between 6.5 and 9 inches long, longer than typical hairdressing scissors. Some are designed with a blunt tip to prevent any injuries due to the dog moving around.

Grooming a dog before it is bathed is important as it frees up and removes dead undercoat and matting and allows proper penetration of water and shampoo to the skin. This can be done by using a slicker brush all over its body, especially on its legs and the places where knotting occurs frequently. Groomers sometimes use a metal comb when combing for the second time, paying more attention to the toes and between the toes. Metal combs can be helpful in the areas of the dog's body that are common spots for knots. Brushing and combing the tail and ears is also important as it is a common area that gets matted more than do the other areas.

Dog brushes come in various sizes and shapes and can be made from metal, plastic, and wood. Although there are many types of dog brushes, the stainless steel wire pin brush and the stainless steel ten-inch poodle comb is what I use on my toy poodles. This comb is the same one that the judges use in dog shows and are great for untangling matted hair.

Finishing touches can be added with finishing supplies, including perfumed sprays, ribbons, and many other accessories.

TOY POODLE CLIPS

BELL-BOTTOM CLIP

Face, neck area, wide bellyband, feet, and base of tail are shaved closely. Topknot and tail are left fluffy and scissored into shape. The legs are left long and fluffy and scissors are used to flair out at the bottom like a bell. The length of hair depends upon your preference.

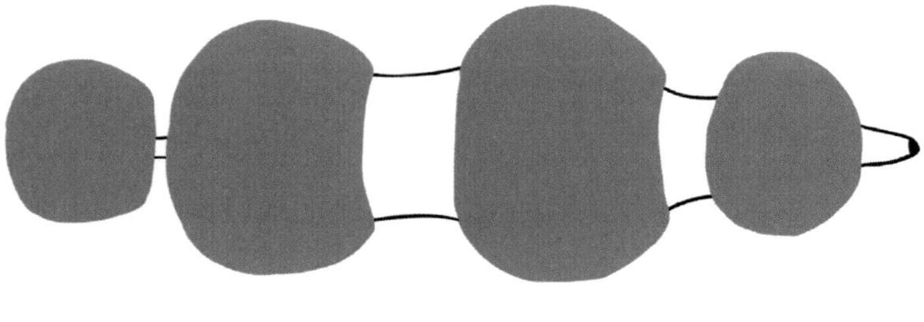

BOLERO CLIP

Face, neck area, bellyband, separation between poms on legs, feet, and base of tail are all shaved closely. The rest of the hair is left fluffy and scissor shaped. Poms on legs are started just above the wrist and hock joints and end just above the feet. A narrow band of 1/2–1 inch is shaved closely between the pom and the rest of the leg hair. The poms are scissor shaped into a round ball shape. The length of hair depends upon your preference.

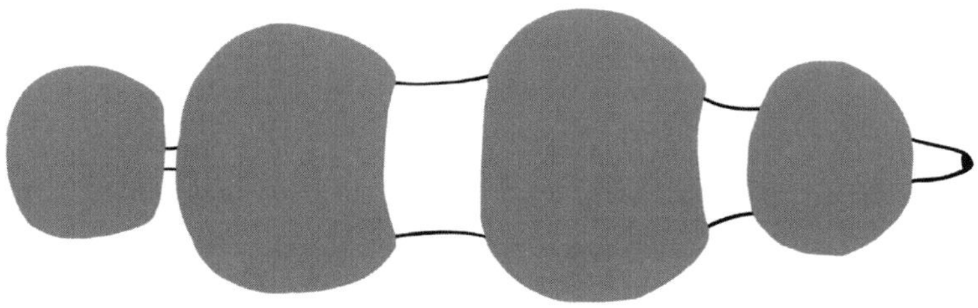

CHICAGO DUTCH CLIP

Face, neck area, bellyband, feet, and base of tail are shaved closely. The bellyband is shaped into a *V*, ending in a narrow line shaved closely along the spine between the hips. The rest of the hair is left fluffy and scissor cut into shape. The length of hair depends upon your preference.

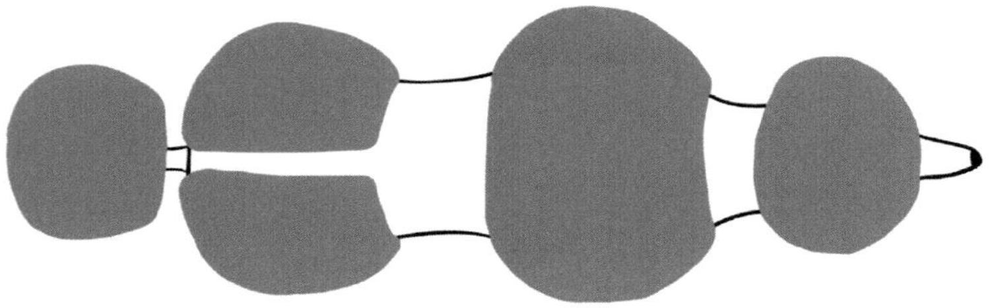

CONTINENTAL CLIP

with Hip Rosettes

Also one of the harder cuts to perform. The face, front legs between poms and elbow, hindquarter to the pom area, and with the exception of the hip rosettes, feet, and base of tail are all shaved very closely. The pack area is left very, very long and scissor shaped. The topknot is left very long and pulled into a ponytail. The tail is left long and scissor shaped into a ball. Poms on the legs are started just above the wrist and hock joints and just above the feet. They are also scissor shaped round. The hip rosettes are placed directly over the hip joint. They are only 1/2–1 inch apart (depending upon the variety of poodle). These are also scissor shaped round. The pack ends 1/2–1 inch behind the last rib. There is only 1/2 inch between the end of the pack and the beginning of the hip rosettes.

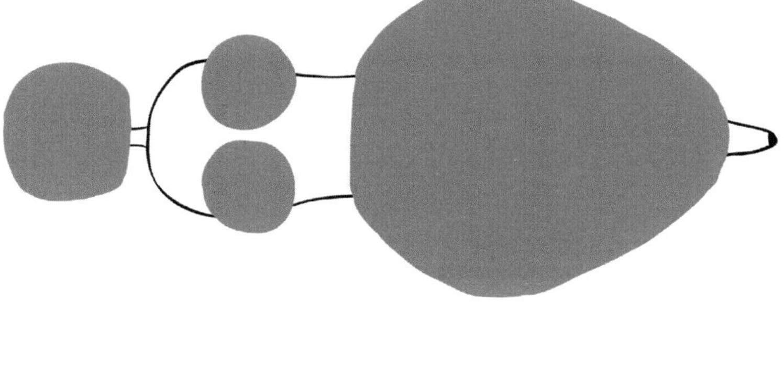

CONTINENTAL CLIP

No Hip Rosettes

Also, one of the harder cuts to perform. The face, front legs between poms and elbow, hindquarter to the pom area and with the exception of the hip rosettes, feet, and base of tail are all shaved very closely. The pack area is left very, very long and scissor shaped. The topknot is left very long and pulled into a ponytail. The tail is left long and scissor shaped into a ball. Poms on the legs are started just above the wrist and hock joints and end just above the feet. They are also scissor shaped round. The only difference between this clip and the other continental clip is that there are no hip rosettes on this clip. This is the most popular cut for the poodles.

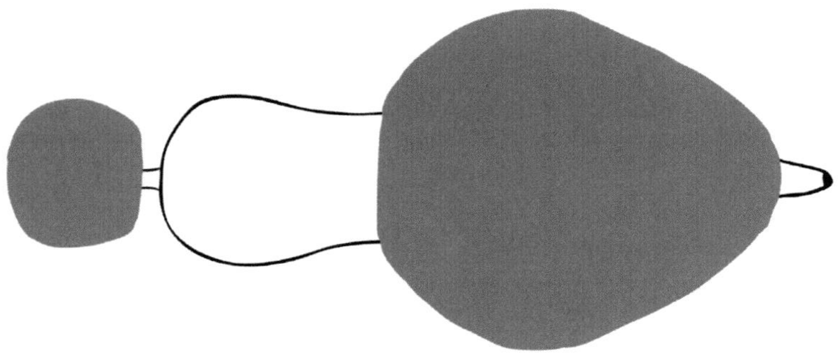

ENGLISH SADDLE CLIP

This cut is very difficult to do and requires a lot of daily grooming. The face, front leg between poms, and tail are shaved close. Poms on front legs start above the wrist joint and ends above the feet. The area over the hips and flanks are scissor shaped shorter into a smooth blanket. Pom on tail is left long and scissor shaped round. The poms on back legs are scissor shaped round and spaced evenly. The bottom pom starts just above the hock and ends above the feet. The other pom starts at the knee area and ends just 1/2–1 1/2 inch (depending upon size of poodle) above the bottom pom.

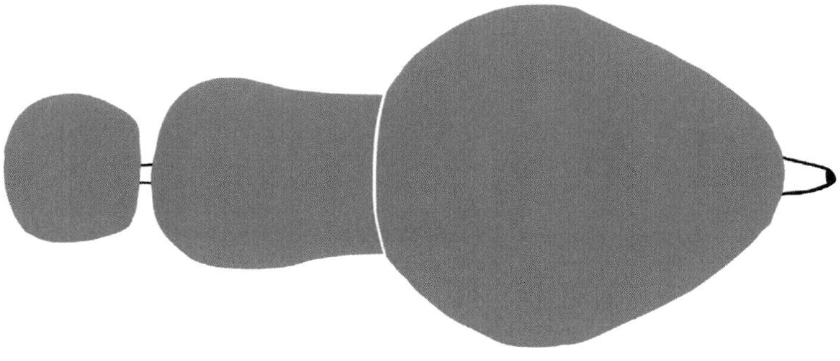

CRISSCROSS DUTCH CLIP

Face, neck area, narrow bellyband, feet, and base of tail are shaved closely. As are the shaved lines between the withers along the spine and between the hips along the spine. These lines are also very narrow. The ends of these lines are left straight. The topknot is scissor shaped into a point at the base of the neck. The rest of the hair is left fluffy and scissor shaped. Length of hair depends upon your preference.

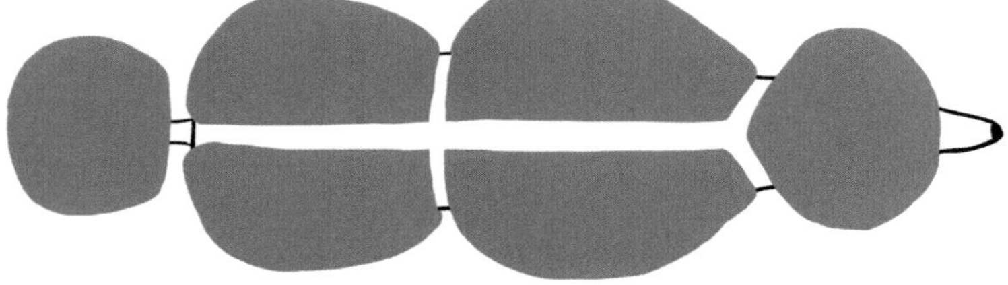

Dutch Clip

Face, neck area, bellyband, feet, and base of tail are shaved closely. As are the lines between the withers along the spine and between the hips along the spine. These lines are very narrow as is the bellyband. Topknot, legs, and tail are left fluffy. This is the longer of the Dutch clip variations. Length of hair depends upon your preference.

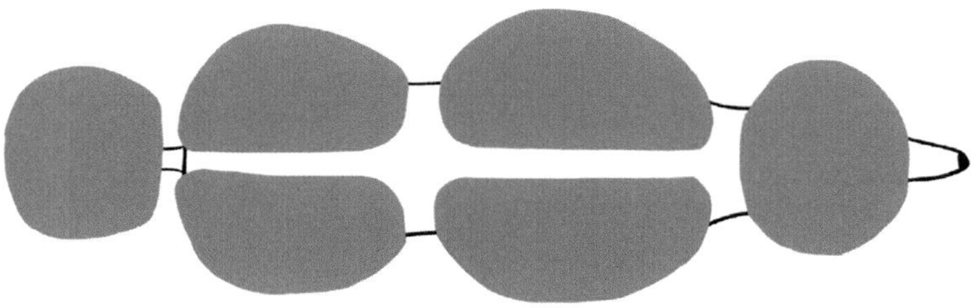

Fifth Avenue Clip

Face, neck area, bellyband, base of tail, feet, and separation between the pack and the pom on the front legs. The pom on the front leg starts just above the wrist joint and ends just above the feet. There should be a shaved narrow separation between the upper part of the leg that is left fluff and the pom at the wrist. Length of body hair depends upon your preference.

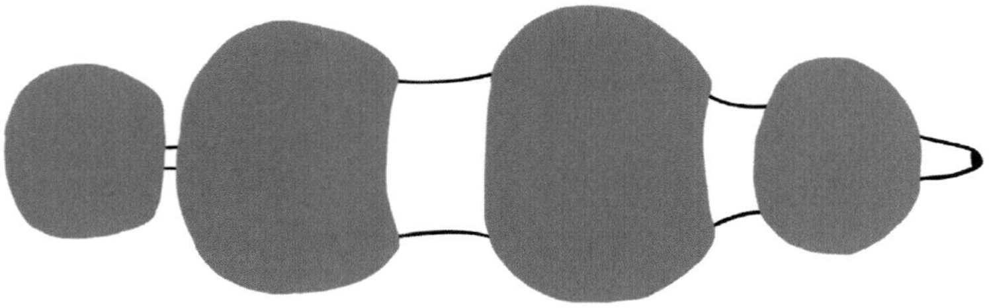

Fox Clip

Face, feet, and tail are shaved closely. There is no pom on the tail. Legs are left longer than the body and rounded. Topknot is fluffy. Length of hair depends upon your preference.

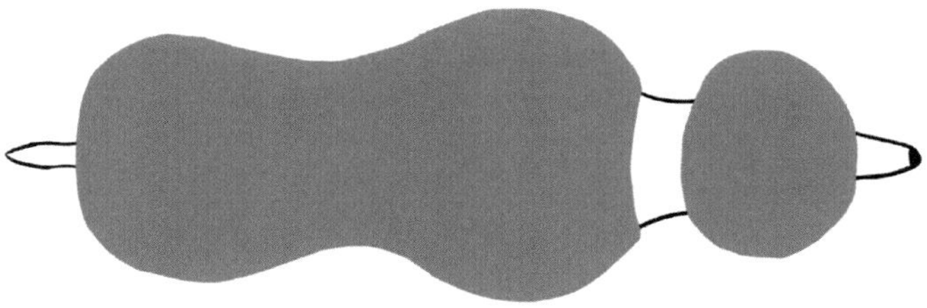

German Clip

Face to corners of the mouth, neck, feet, and whole tail are shaved closely. There is no pom on the tail. The ears are also completely shaved in this cut. Head and body are left fluffy and scissor shaped into classic lines.

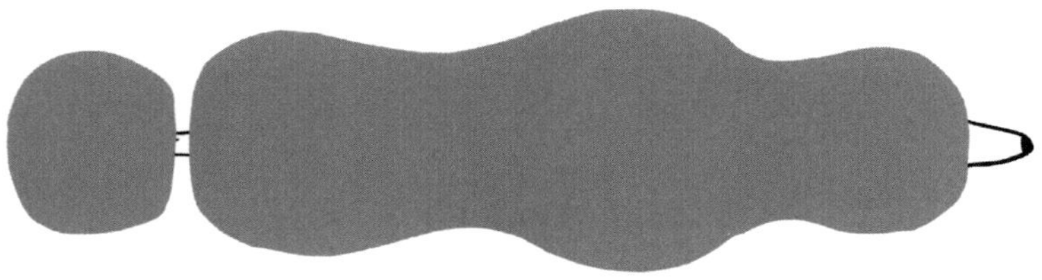

German Clip Variation

This is a variation of the German clip. The only difference being that the feet are not shaved in this clip.

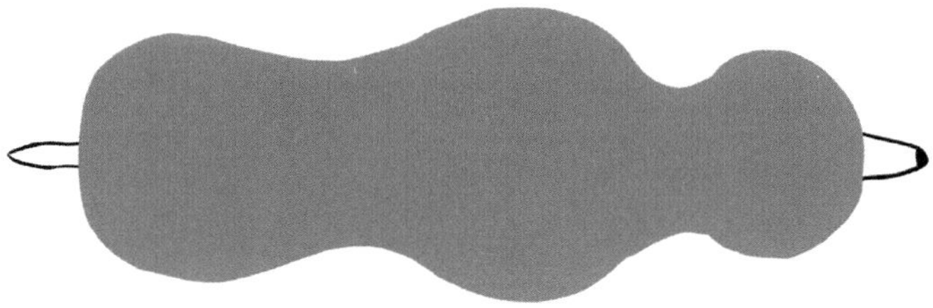

JACKET AND PANTS CLIP

Face, neck area, body, feet, and base of tail are shaved closely. The legs, topknot, and tail are left fluffy and are scissor shaped round. Length of the legs depends upon your preference.

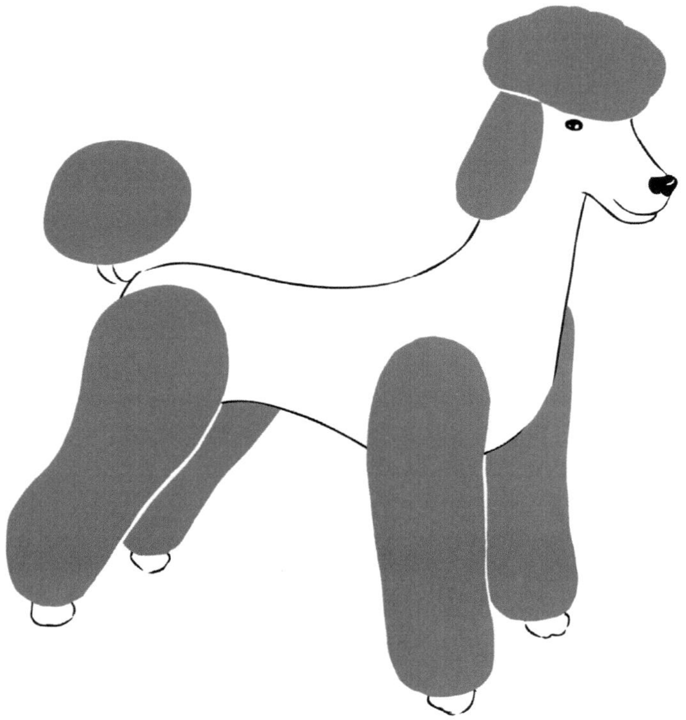

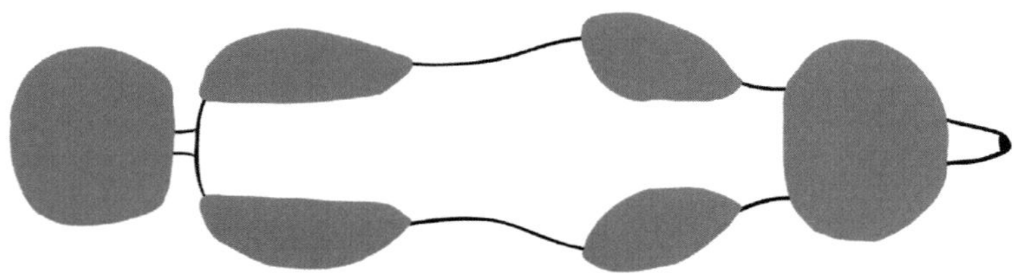

LAMB CLIP (SHOW)

Face, feet, and base of tail are shaved closely. Legs are left fluffy along with the tail and topknot. Body can be shaved with a larger blade or scissor shaped to be shorter than the legs. Length of hair depends upon your preference.

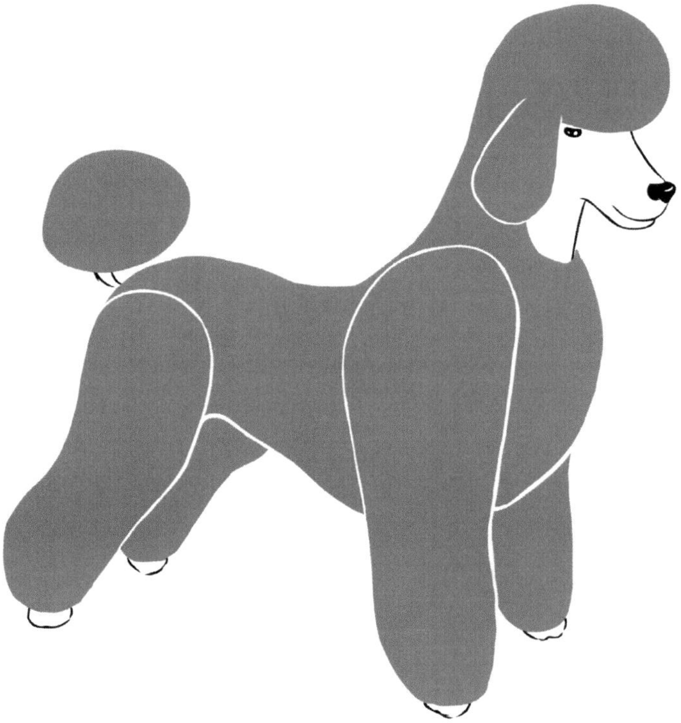

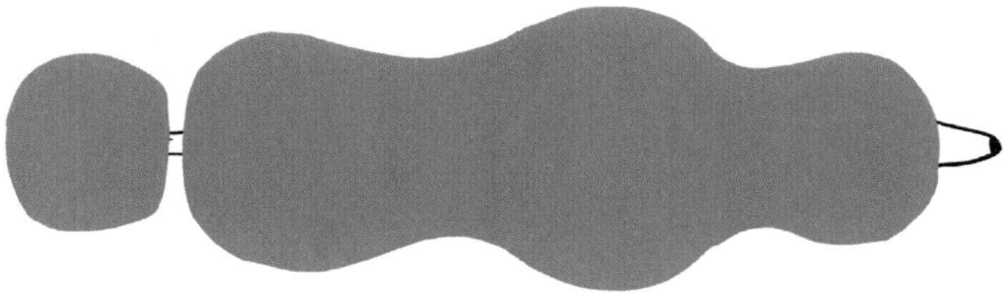

Lion Clip (Pet)

Face, neck area, hindquarters, back legs to the pom area, front legs from the elbow to the pom area, feet, and base of tail are shaved closely. Poms on legs are started just above the wrist and hock joints and end just above the feet. These poms are scissor shaped round. The tail and head are left fluffy. The pack is left fluffy and just scissor shaped. The length of pack area depends upon your preference.

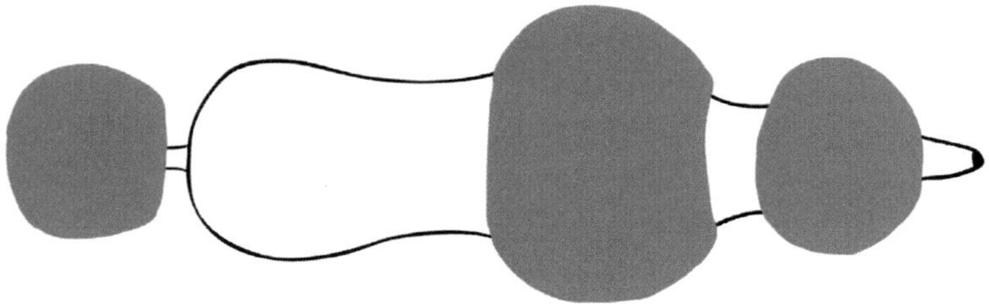

Miami Clip

Face, feet, and base of tail are shaved closely. Body hair is left fluffy but not too long and then scissor shaped. The legs are scissor shaped into a pom at the bottom, starting just above the wrist and the hock ending just above the feet. Length of hair depends upon your preference.

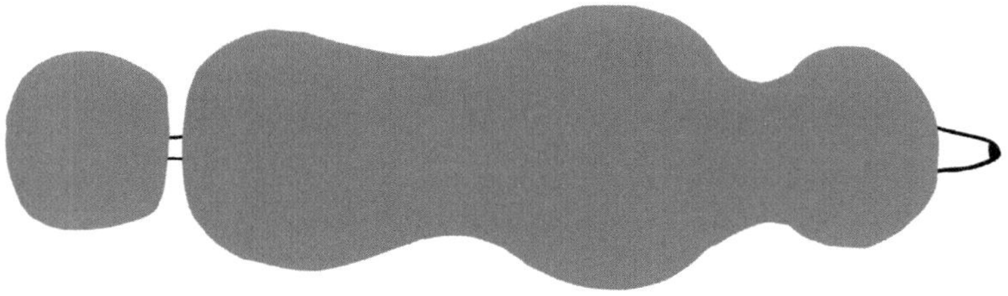

Miami Clip Variation

Face, neck area, hindquarters, back legs to the pom area, front legs from the elbow to the pom area, feet, and base of tail are shaved closely. Poms on legs are started just above the wrist and hock joints and just above the feet. These poms are scissor shaped round. The tail and head are left fluffy. The pack is left fluffy and just scissor shaped. Length of pack area depends upon your preference.

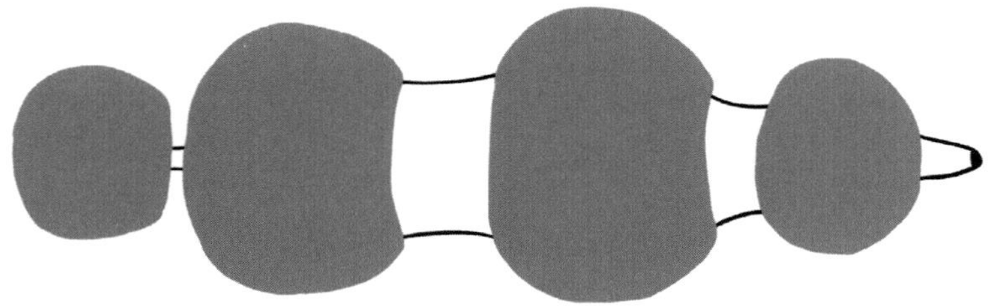

New Yorker Clip

Face, neck area, a wide bellyband, feet, and base of tail are shaved closely. The body hair is left fluffy and scissor shaped. There are no lines shaved along the spine in this cut. Length of body hair depends upon your preference.

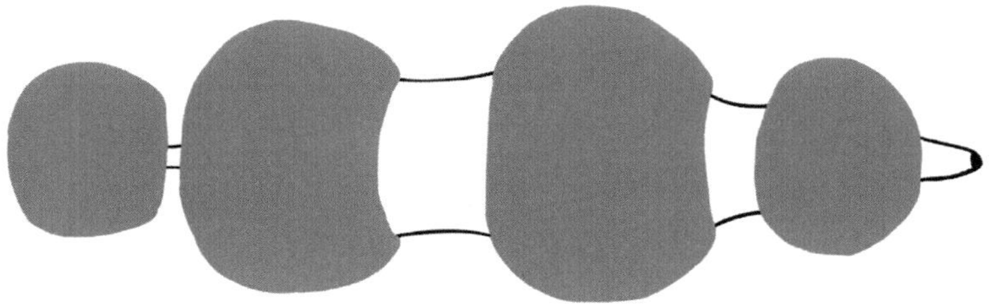

Pittsburgh Dutch Clip

Face, neck area, feet, bellyband, and base of tail are shaved closely. A line is shaved between the withers following the spine to the bellyband. There is no line shaved between the hips along the spine. The rest of the body hair and topknot are left fluffy. Hair length depends upon your preference

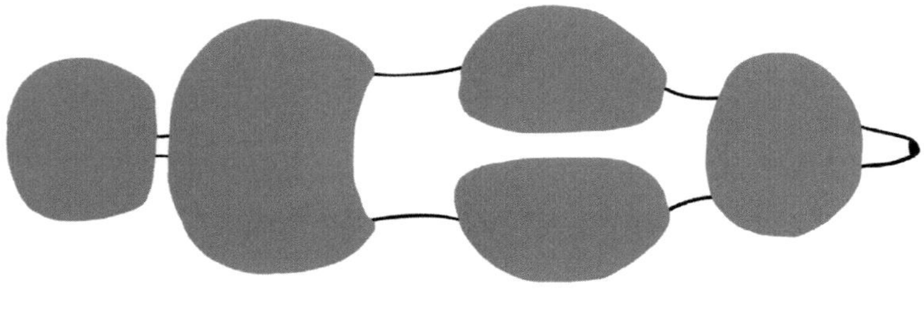

Puppy Clip (Pet)

Face, feet, and base of tail are shaved closely. The rest of the body is scissor shaped to follow the flow of the dog. This cut is not left as long as the show puppy cut. Length of body hair depends upon your preference. Topknot is left fluffy but not long enough to pull into a ponytail.

Puppy Clip (Show)

Face, feet, and base of tail are shaved closely. Body is left long and shaped to complement the dog's form. The pack is shaped into the neck and topknot. The topknot is left long and pulled into a ponytail. This is an AKC approved show cut for poodles under one year and a UKC show cut for poodles of any age.

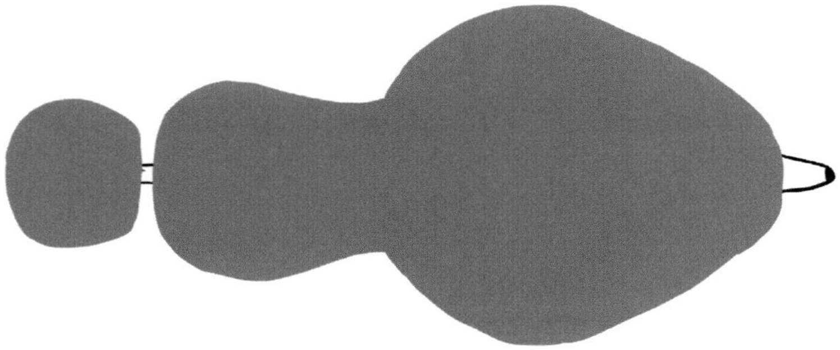

Retriever Clip

Face, feet, and base of tail are shaved closely. Body hair is short all over and just scissor shaped. Topknot and tail are left longer than the body hair. This is a great clip for summer and is very easy to take care of. Length of body hair depends upon your preference and what blade is used. Usually a 4, 5, or 7 blade is used in this cut.

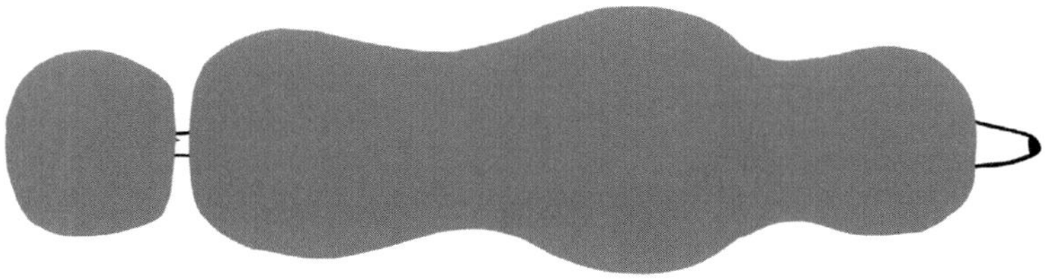

Sporting Clip

Face, feet, and base of tail are shaved closely. The body is left fluffy and scissor shaped. Length of hair depends upon your preference, although it is to be longer rather than shorter. This clip is AKC approved for agility and obedience events. UKC allows this clip in the conformation ring.

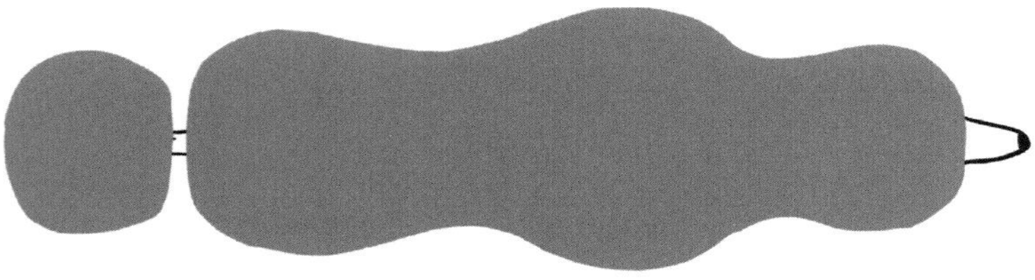

Swirl Clip

Face, feet, and base of tail are shaved closely. A *Y* shape is shaved closely between the pack and the hips along the spine with the arms of the *Y* ending down the sides and curving into a swirl that end in a point at the start of the flanks. Swirl may go either direction. Body hair is left fluffy. Length of hair depends upon preference. This clip is much like the Y clip.

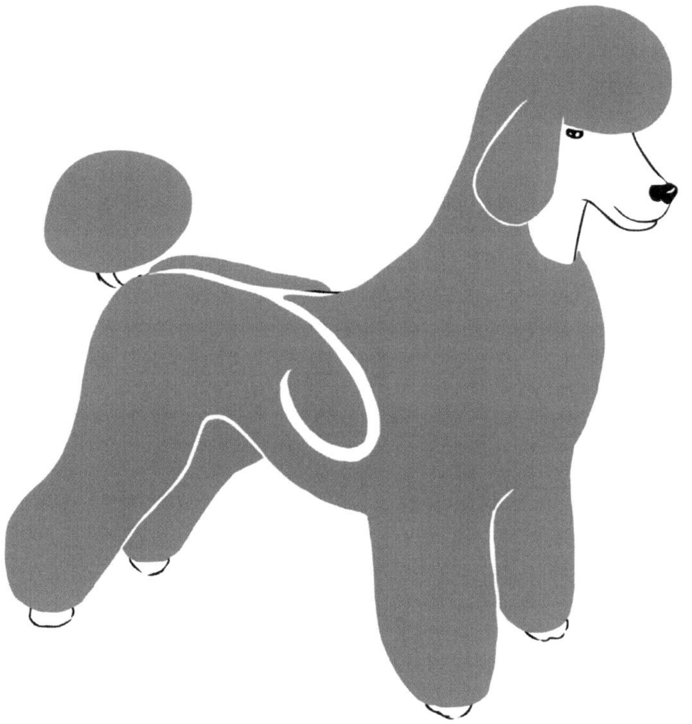

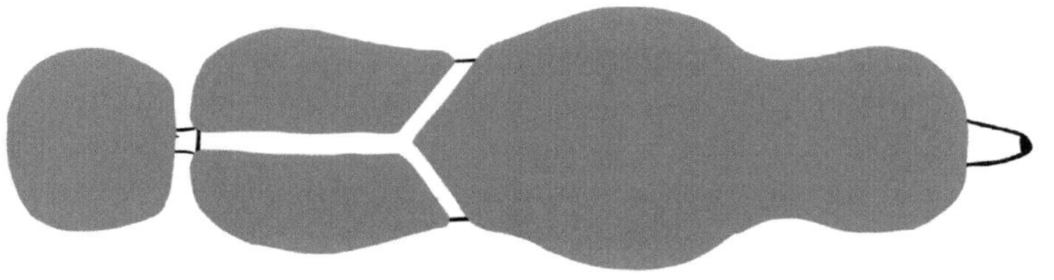

Teddy Bear Clip

In this clip, the hair is left fluffy all over. The face is not shaved, but the facial hair is scissor cut away from the eyes and the rest is rounded. The feet may or may not be shaved in this cut as is the same with the base of the tail. The body hair is all rounded to give the poodle more of a bichon look to them. Length of hair depends upon your preference.

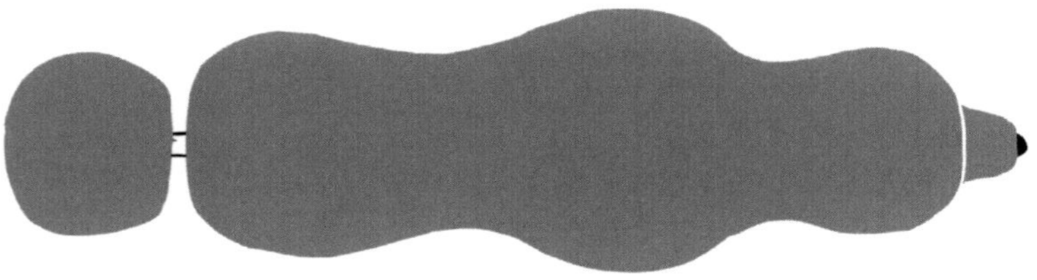

T Clip

Face, feet, and base of tail are shaved closely. Body is scissor shape. Topknot is left longer but is not pulled into a ponytail. Length of body hair depends upon your preference.

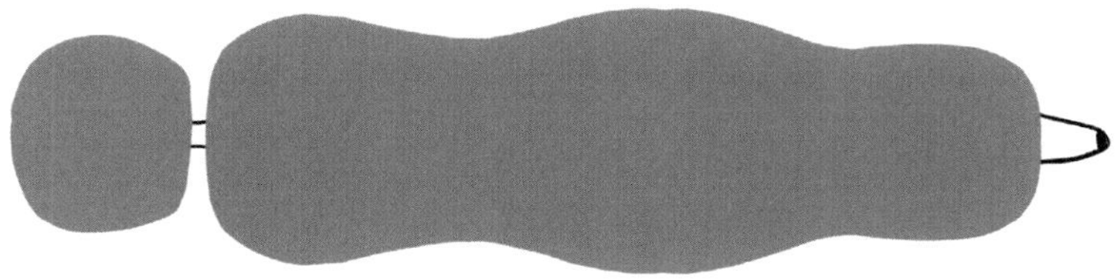

Town and Country Clip

Face, neck area, wide bellyband, feet, and base of tail are shaved closely. Also, there are narrow lines shaved closely between the whither along the spine into the bellyband and also between the hips along the spine into the bellyband. The rest of the hair is left fluffy and scissor shaped, with the edges of the lines are curved. Length of body hair depends upon your preference.

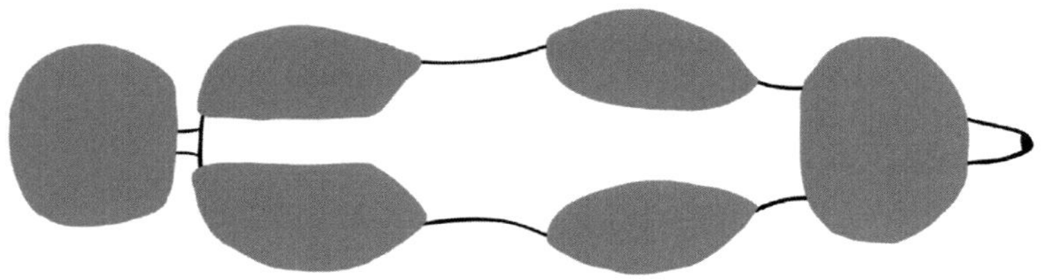

Y Clip

Face, feet, and base of tail are shaved closely. There is a *Y* shape shaved closely into the coat between the pack and the hips along the spine area and spreading out into the arms of the *Y*. The arms of the *Y* end in a point where the flank starts. The rest of the body is left fluffy. Length of hair depends upon your preference.

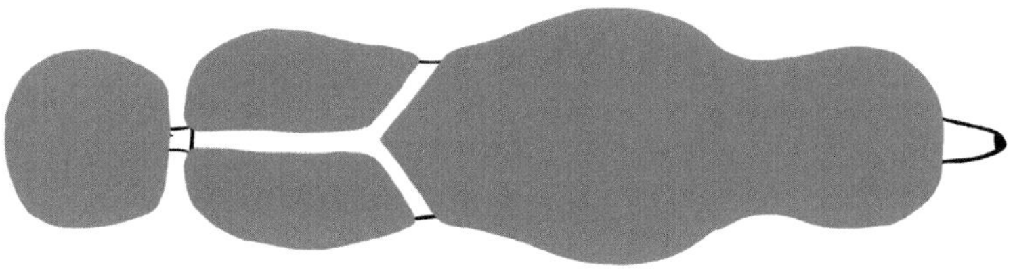

AKC COLOR CODES FOR POODLES

Description	Code
Apricot	002
Black	007
Black & Apricot	246
Black & Brown	009
Black & Cream	010
Black & Gray	012
Black & Red	014
Black & Silver	016
Black & White	019
Blue	037
Blue & White	045
Brown (mahogany, dark walnut or chestnut)	061
Brown & Apricot	247
Brown & White	063
Cafe Au Lait	069
Cream	076
Cream & White	077
Gray	100
Gray & White	105
Red	140
Red & Apricot	157
Red & White	146
Silver	176
Silver Beige	183
White	199
White & Apricot	200
White & Silver	216

AKC BREED STANDARD

Adopted by the Poodle Club of America Inc. and approved by the American Kennel Club.

General Appearance, Carriage, and Condition

That of a very active, intelligent, and elegant-appearing dog, squarely built, well proportioned, moving soundly, and carrying himself proudly. Properly clipped in the traditional fashion and carefully groomed, the poodle has about him an air of distinction and dignity peculiar to himself.

Size, Proportion, Substance

The standard poodle is over fifteen inches at the highest point of the shoulders. Any poodle that is fifteen inches or less in height shall be disqualified from competition as a standard poodle.

The miniature poodle is fifteen inches or under at the highest point of the shoulders, with a minimum height in excess of ten inches. Any poodle that is over fifteen inches or is ten inches or less at the highest point of the shoulders shall be disqualified from competition as a miniature poodle.

The toy poodle is ten inches or under at the highest point of the shoulders. Any poodle that is more than ten inches at the highest point of the shoulders shall be disqualified from competition as a toy poodle.

As long as the toy poodle is definitely a toy poodle and the miniature poodle a miniature poodle, both in balance and proportion for the variety, diminutiveness shall be the deciding factor when all other points are equal.

Proportion: to ensure the desirable squarely built appearance, the length of body measured from the breastbone to the point of the rump approximates the height from the highest point of the shoulders to the ground.

Substance: bone and muscle of both forelegs and hind legs are in proportion to size of dog.

Head and Expression

a. Eyes - very dark, oval in shape, and set far enough apart and positioned to create an alert intelligent expression. Major fault: eyes round, protruding, large or very light.

b. Ears - hanging close to the head, set at or slightly below eye level. The ear leather is long, wide, and thickly feathered; however, the ear fringe should not be of excessive length.

c. Skull - moderately rounded, with a slight but definite stop. The cheekbones and muscles flat. Length from occiput to stop about the same as length of muzzle.

d. Muzzle - long, straight, and fine, with slight chiseling under the eyes. Strong without lippiness. The chin definite enough to preclude snippiness, which results in major faults: lack of chin, teeth—white, strong, and with a scissors bite. Major fault: undershot, overshot, wry mouth.

Neck, Topline, Body

Neck well proportioned, strong and long enough to permit the head to be carried high and with dignity. Skin snug at throat. The neck rises from strong, smoothly muscled shoulders. Major fault: ere the neck. [Note: missing words to complete sentence thought] The topline is level, neither sloping nor ranched, from the highest point of the shoulder blade to the base of the tail, with the exception of a slight hollow just behind the shoulder.

Body

a. Chest deep and moderately wide with well-sprung ribs.
b. The loin is short, broad and muscular.
c. Tail straight, set on high and carried up, docked of sufficient length to ensure a balanced out line. Major fault: set low, curled, or carried over the back.

Forequarters

Strong, smoothly muscled shoulders. The shoulder blade is well laid-back and approximately the same length as the upper foreleg. Major fault: steep shoulder.
Forelegs straight and parallel when viewed from the front. When viewed from the side, the elbow is directly below the highest point of the shoulder. The pasterns are strong. Dewclaws may be removed.

Feet

The feet are rather small, oval in shape, with toes well arched and cushioned on thick firm pads. Nails short but not excessively shortened. The feet turn neither in nor out. Major fault: paper or splay foot.

Hindquarters

The angulation of the hindquarters balances that of the forequarters.

Hind legs straight and parallel when viewed from the rear. Muscular with width in the region of the stifles, which are well bent; femur and tibia are about equal in length; hock to heel short and perpendicular to the ground. When standing, the rear toes are only slightly behind the point of the rump. Major fault: cow-hocks.

Coat

a. Quality - 1. Curly: of naturally harsh texture, dense throughout. 2. Corded: hanging in tight even cords of varying length; longer on mane or body coat, head, and ears; shorter on puffs, bracelets, and pompons.
b. Clip - A poodle under twelve months may be shown in the puppy clip. In all regular classes, poodles twelve months or over must be shown in the English Saddle or Continental clip. In the Stud Dog and Brood Bitch classes and in a noncompetitive Parade of Champions, poodles may be shown in the sporting clip. A poodle shown in any other type of clip shall be disqualified.

1. Puppy - A poodle under a year old may be shown in the puppy clip with the coat long. The face, throat, feet, and base of the tail are shaved. The entire shaven foot is visible. There is a pompon on the end of the tail. In order to give a neat appearance and a smooth unbroken line, shaping of the coat is permissible.
2. English Saddle - In the English Saddle clip, the face, throat, feet, forelegs, and base of the tail are shaved, leaving puffs on the forelegs and a pompon on the end of the tail. The hind

quarters are covered with a short blanket of hair except for a curved shaved area on each flank and two shaved bands on each hind leg. The entire shaven foot and a portion of the shaven leg above the puff are visible. The rest of the body is left in full coat but may be shaped in order to insure overall balance.

3. Continental - In the Continental clip, the face, throat, feet, and base of the tail are shaved. The hindquarters are shaved with pompons (optional) on the hips. The legs are shaved, leaving bracelets on the hind legs and puffs on the forelegs. There is a pompon on the end of the tail. The entire shaven foot and a portion of the shaven foreleg above the puff are visible. The rest of the body is left in full coat but may be shaped in order to insure overall balance.
4. Sporting - In the Sporting clip, a poodle shall be shown with face, feet, throat, and base of tail shaved, leaving a scissor cap on the top of the head and a pompon on the end of the tail. The rest of the body and legs are clipped or scissored to follow the outline of the dog, leaving a short blanket of coat no longer than one inch in length. The hair on the legs may be slightly longer than that on the body.

In all clips, the hair of the topknot may be left free or held in place by elastic bands. The hair is only of sufficient length to present a smooth outline. *Topknot* refers only to hair on the skull, from stop to occiput. This is the only area where elastic bands may be used.

Color

The coat is an even and solid color at the skin. In blues, grays, silvers, browns, cafe au laits, apricots, and creams, the coat may show varying shades of the same color. This is frequently present in the somewhat darker feathering of the ears and in the tipping of the ruff. While clear colors are definitely preferred, such natural variation in the shading of the coat is not to be considered a fault. Brown and cafe-au-lait poodles have liver-colored noses, eye-rims, and lips; dark toenails; and dark amber eyes. Black, blue, gray, silver, cream, and white poodles have black noses, eye-rims, and lips; black or self-colored toenails; and very dark eyes. In the apricots while the foregoing coloring is preferred, liver-colored noses, eye-rims, and lips and amber eyes are permitted but are not desirable. Major fault: color of nose, lips, and eye-rims incomplete, or of wrong color for color of dog.

Parti-colored dogs shall be disqualified. The coat of a parti-colored dog is not an even solid color at the skin but is of two or more colors.

Gait

A straightforward trot with light springy action and strong hindquarters drive. Head and tail carried up. Sound effortless movement is essential.

Temperament

Carrying himself proudly, very active, intelligent, the poodle has about him an air of distinction and dignity peculiar to himself. Major fault: shyness or sharpness.

Major Faults

Any distinct deviation from the desired characteristics described in the breed standard.

Disqualifications

Size - A dog over or under the height limits specified shall be disqualified.
Clip - A dog in any type of clip other than those listed under coat shall be disqualified.
Parti-colors - The coat of a parti-colored dog is not an even solid color at the skin but of two or more colors. Parti-colored dogs shall be disqualified.

Value of Points

General appearance, temperament, carriage, and condition	30
Head, expression, ears, eyes, and teeth	20
Body, neck, legs, feet, and tail	20
Gait	20
Coat, color, and texture	10

Approved August 14, 1984
Reformatted March 27, 1990

PUPPY DOG SHOWS—AKC STANDARD

The World of Dog Shows

Showing dogs is a great sport where the thrill of competition is combined with the joy of seeing beautiful dogs. Dog shows are one of many types of AKC dog events in which AKC registered dogs can compete. These events, which draw over three million entries annually, include dog shows and tests of instinct and trainability, such as obedience trials, Canine Good Citizen tests, field trials, agility trials, lure coursing, rally, hunting tests, herding trials, tracking tests, coonhound, and earth dog events.

Dog shows (conformation events) are intended to evaluate breeding stock. The size of these events ranges from large all-breed shows, with over 3,000 dogs entered, to small local specialty club shows, featuring a specific breed. The dog's conformation (overall appearance and structure), an indication of the dog's ability to produce quality puppies, is judged.

Types of Conformation Dog Shows

All-breed shows offer competitions for over 150 breeds and varieties of dogs recognized by the AKC. All-breed shows are the type often shown on television

Specialty shows are restricted to dogs of a specific breed or to varieties of one breed. For example, the Bulldog Club of America Specialty is for bulldogs only, but the Poodle Club of America's specialty show includes the three varieties of the poodle—standard, miniature, and toy.

Group shows are limited to dogs belonging to one of the seven groups. For example, the Potomac Hound Group show features only breeds belonging to the hound group.

WHICH DOGS MAY PARTICIPATE

To be Eligible to Compete, a Dog Must:

Be individually registered with the American Kennel Club
Be six months of age or older
Be a breed for which classes are offered at a show
Meet any eligibility requirements in the written standard for its breed

Spayed or neutered dogs are not eligible to compete in conformation classes at a dog show because the purpose of a dog show is to evaluate breeding stock.

The Role of the Judge

Judges examine the dogs, then give awards according to how closely each dog compares to the judge's mental image of the "perfect" dog described in the breed's official standard.

The standard describes the characteristics that allow the breed to perform the function for which it was bred. These standards include specifications for structure, temperament, and movement.

The official written standard for each breed is maintained by the breed's national club and is included in *The Complete Dog Book* published by the AKC.

The judges are experts on the breeds they are judging. They examine (go over) each dog with their hands to see if the teeth, muscles, bones, and coat texture conform to the breed's standard. They view each dog in profile for overall balance and watch each dog gait (move) to see how all of those features fit together in action.

HOW A DOG SHOW WORKS

Each dog presented to a judge is exhibited (handled) by its owner, breeder, or a hired professional. The role of a handler is similar to that of a jockey who rides a horse around the track and, hopefully, into the winner's circle.

Most dogs in competition at conformation shows are competing for points toward their AKC championships. It takes fifteen points, including two majors (wins of three, four, or five points) awarded by at least three different judges to become an American Kennel Club Champion of Record.

The number of championship points awarded at a show depends on the number of males (dogs) and females (bitches) of the breed actually in competition. The larger the entry, the greater the number of points a male or a female can win. The maximum number of points awarded to a dog at any show is five points.

Males and females compete separately within their respective breeds in seven regular classes. The following classes are offered and are divided by sex:

Puppy - For dogs between six and twelve months of age that are not yet champions (optional class).

Twelve-to-eighteen months - For dogs twelve to eighteen months of age that are not yet champions (optional class).

Novice - For dogs six months of age and over, which have not, prior to the date of closing of entries, won three first prizes in the Novice Class, a first prize in Breed-by-Exhibitor, American-Breed, or Open Classes, nor one or more points toward their championship (optional class).

Amateur owner-handler - For dogs that are at least six months of age that are not champions. Dogs must be handled in the class by the registered owner of the dog and is limited to exhibitors who have not, at any point in time, been a professional dog handler, AKC approved conformation judge, or employed as an assistant to a professional handler (effective January 1, 2009) (optional class).

Breed by exhibitor - For dogs that are exhibited by their owner and breeder that are not yet champions (optional class).

American bred - For dogs born in the United States from a mating that took place in the United States that are not yet champions (mandatory class).

Open - For any dog of the breed, at least six months of age (mandatory class).
After these classes are judged, all the dogs that won first place in a class compete again to see who is the best of the winning dogs. Males and females are judged separately. Only the best male (Winners Dog) and the best female (Winners Bitch) receive championship points. The Winners Dog and Winners Bitch then compete with the champions for the Best of Breed award. At the end of the Best of Breed Competition, three awards are usually given:

Best of Breed - the dog judged as the best in its breed category.

Best of Winners - the dog judged as the better of the Winners Dog and Winners Bitch.
Best of Opposite Sex - the best dog that is the opposite sex to the Best of Breed winner.

The Road to Best in Show

Dog shows are a process of elimination, with one dog being named Best in Show at the end of the show.

Only the Best of Breed winners advance to compete in the group competitions. Each AKC-recognized breed falls into one of seven group classifications. The seven groups are sporting, hound, working, terrier, toy, nonsporting, and herding. Four placements are awarded in each group, but only the first-place winner advances to the Best in Show competition.

The Seven Groups in All-Breed Shows

Sporting - These dogs were bred to hunt game birds both on land and in the water. The breeds in this group include pointers, retrievers, setters, and spaniels.

Hounds - These breeds were bred for hunting other game by sight or scent. These breeds include such dogs as beagles, bassets, dachshunds, and greyhounds.

Working - These dogs were bred to pull carts, guard property, and perform search and rescue services. Among the breeds in this group are the Akita, boxer, Doberman pinscher, and St. Bernard.

Terrier - This group includes breeds such as the Airedale, cairn terrier, and Scottish terrier. Terriers were bred to rid property of vermin such as rats.

Toy - These dogs were bred to be household companions. This group includes little dogs such as the Chihuahua, Maltese, Pomeranian, and pug.

Nonsporting - This diverse group includes the chow, bulldog, dalmatian, and poodle. These dogs vary in size and function, and many are considered companion dogs.

Herding - These dogs were bred to help shepherds and ranchers herd their livestock. The border, collie, German shepherd dog, and Old English sheepdog are some of the breeds in this group.

Finally, the seven group winners are brought into the ring where they compete for Best in Show, the highest award at a dog show.

Ribbons

Each dog that receives an award is given a ribbon by the judge. The color of the ribbon indicates the type of award the dog has won.

Blue - awarded for first place in any regular class. Also awarded to the winner of each group competition, usually in the form of a rosette.

Red - awarded for second place in each class. Also awarded for second place in each group competition, usually in the form of a rosette.

Yellow - awarded for third place in each class. Also awarded for third place in each group competition, usually in the form of a rosette.

White - awarded for fourth place in each class. Also awarded for fourth place of each group competition, usually in the form of a rosette.

Purple - awarded to the winners of the Winners Dog and Winners Bitch classes. Since these are the classes in which championship points are earned, these ribbons are highly coveted.

Purple and White - awarded to the Reserve Winners; that is, the runners-up to the winner of the Winners Dog and Winners Bitch classes.

Blue and White - awarded to the dog that wins Best of Winners; that is, the better of the Winners Dog and Winners Bitch winners.

Purple and Gold - awarded to the dog judged "Best of Breed" in each breed competition. This is highly coveted because it allows advancement to the Group competition.

Red and White - awarded to the Best of Opposite Sex. This means the best dog of the breed that is the opposite sex of the Best of Breed winner.

Red, White, and Blue - only one of these is awarded at the end of each show. It is given to the ultimate award winner, the Best in Show.

HOW DO I GET STARTED SHOWING MY DOG?

The best place to start is by joining a local club, whether an all-breed kennel club or a breed-specific specialty club. A listing of clubs by state can be found on our AKC search page (AKC.com) or through the customer service department by calling (919) 233-9767.

Local clubs will have information on training classes for the show ring and for obedience and agility classes. Even if the show ring is not your ultimate goal, the relationship that training forms between you and your dog will be very rewarding to you both. Local clubs also have matches where you and your dog can test your skill in the ring.

Handling your dog is an exceptional and enjoyable experience. From the grooming table to the show ring, you and your dog will develop a bond. While training classes offer the best hands-on way to practice for the show ring, attending shows and observing your breed is also a great way to gain understanding of what judges and other competitors do.

If you do not wish to handle your dog yourself or have a friend or family member do it, you may contact a professional handler who charges a fee for showing your dog.

You're on your way! You are entering a sport that will bring many hours of enjoyment and education to every member of your family. You will make many friends in the sport and will enjoy your dog and your new hobby for many years to come.

Junior Showmanship

The AKC offers children nine to eighteen years of age the opportunity to compete with others their own age at various AKC events. Juniors competing in conformation events are judged on how they present their dogs.

Tips for the First-Time Exhibitor

Make sure your dog is registered with the AKC.
Be sure your dog is current on all inoculations.
Learn the proper techniques for grooming and for presenting your dog in the ring.
Join your breed's Parent Club or a Local Specialty and/or All-Breed club in your area.
Become familiar with the AKC rules and regulations for dog shows.
Attend some dog shows to observe your breed being judged and how others present your breed.
Get a judging program at the show to find out ring number and judging time.
Use the knowledge of your breeder.
Don't be afraid to ask questions.
Attend handling classes with your dog.

Clips for the First-Time Spectator

If the grooming area is open to spectators, visit it and talk with professional groomers to get tips on keeping your dog looking his best.

However tempting, do not pet a dog without asking for permission first. The dog may have just been groomed in preparation for being judged.

At each dog show, you will find vendors and information booths. Many club booths offer helpful information to the general public.

Wear comfortable shoes, you'll be doing a lot of walking. Unless you bring a chair or arrive early, be prepared to stand most of the time, as seating is usually limited.

If you are considering getting a purebred dog, talk to the breeders and exhibitors—they are experts in their breeds

If you bring a baby stroller to a dog show, be careful that you do not run over any dog's tail and that your child does not grab or poke the dogs it can reach. Avoid having them near ring entrances, which are especially crowded. Some shows prohibit baby strollers.

DOG SHOW TERMS

Angulation -	Angles created by bones meeting at their joints.
Baiting -	Using liver or some treat to get the dog's attention and have him look alert.
Bench show -	A dog show at which the dogs are kept on assigned benches when not being shown in competition, so they can be viewed and discussed by attendees, exhibitors, and breeders.
Exhibitor -	A person who brings a dog to a dog show and shows it in the appropriate class.
Fancier -	A person who is especially interested and usually active in some phase of the sport of purebred dogs.
Gait -	The way a dog moves, movement is a good indicator of structure and condition.
Groom -	To brush, comb, trim, or otherwise make a dog's coat neat.
Handler -	A person or agent who takes a dog into the show ring or who works the dog at a field trial or other performance event.
Heel -	A command to a dog to keep close beside its handler.
Match show -	A usually informal dog show at which no championship points are awarded.
Miscellaneous class -	Transitional class for breeds attempting to advance to full AKC recognition.
Pedigree -	The written record of a dog's family tree of three or more generations.
Points -	Credits earned toward a championship.
Soundness -	Mental and physical well-being.
Stacking -	Posing the dog's legs and body to create a pleasing picture.

CPSIA information can be obtained
at www.ICGtesting.com
Printed in the USA
LVIC04n1654260814
401011LV00014B/95

* 9 7 8 1 6 2 2 9 5 8 1 0 8 *